STUDY GUIDE

FINISH
FINANCIALLY
⟶ FREE

Copyright © 2023 by Kristi Service Nowrouzi

Published by Kudu Publishing

All rights reserved. No portion of this book may be reproduced, stored in a retrieval system, or transmitted in any form or by any means—electronic, mechanical, photocopy, recording, scanning, or other—except for brief quotations in critical reviews or articles, without prior written permission of the author.
For foreign and subsidiary rights, contact the author.

NMLS #754092 Equal Housing Opportunity

Cover design by Sara Young
Cover Photo by Andrew van Tilborgh

ISBN: 978-1-959095-96-5   1 2 3 4 5 6 7 8 9 10

Printed in the United States of America

STUDY GUIDE

FINISH FINANCIALLY ⟶ FREE

KRISTI SERVICE NOWROUZI

CONTENTS

Chapter 1. My Story 6

Chapter 2. Our Beliefs Are the Problem 10

Chapter 3. Habits We Have Formed 16

Chapter 4. Couples and Money 20

Chapter 5. Money Personalities 26

Chapter 6. Psychology in Money 30

Chapter 7. The Broke Trap 34

Chapter 8. Financial Literacy—The Basics 38

Chapter 9. Run Your Numbers Like You're a Business 42

Chapter 10. Credit 48

Chapter 11. Debt Repayment 52

Chapter 12. Consider Your Future 56

Chapter 13. Action Plan 60

Personal Monthly Budget 68

IDENTIFY YOUR MONEY BELIEFS
MASTER YOUR MONEY
LIVE IN ABUNDANCE

FINISH FINANCIALLY ➡ FREE

KRISTI SERVICE NOWROUZI

CHAPTER 1

MY STORY

Let's stop getting our butts kicked. Finally.

READING TIME

As you read Chapter 1: "My Story" in Finish Financially Free, review, reflect on, and respond to the text by answering the following questions.

REFLECT AND TAKE ACTION:

What's your financial story?

_____
_____
_____
_____
_____
_____
_____
_____
_____
_____
_____

What main aspects of this chapter can you relate to?

_____
_____
_____
_____
_____
_____
_____
_____
_____
_____
_____

How would you describe your current relationship with money?

_____
_____
_____
_____
_____
_____
_____
_____
_____
_____
_____

What is your ultimate financial goal?

_____
_____
_____
_____
_____
_____
_____
_____
_____
_____
_____
_____
_____

What are you willing to change to reach your financial goal(s)?

CHAPTER 2

OUR BELIEFS ARE THE PROBLEM

Having the wrong beliefs about money keep us stuck and broke.

READING TIME

As you read Chapter 2: "Our Beliefs Are the Problem" in *Finish Financially Free*, review, reflect on, and respond to the text by answering the following questions.

REFLECT AND TAKE ACTION:

Do you think you have any improper perspectives, misguided direction or limiting beliefs when it comes to money, spending, and finances? What are they?

_____
_____
_____
_____
_____
_____
_____
_____
_____

Where or from whom do you think you got those beliefs from about money, spending and finances?

_____
_____
_____
_____
_____
_____
_____
_____
_____

Why is it important to look at our beliefs instead of only our actions?

___

When you think of money, what is the first thing that comes to mind?

___

Did money cause stress in your family growing up? What about in your life currently? How do you think this has altered your view of money?

_____
_____
_____
_____
_____
_____
_____

What did your father think about money?

_____
_____
_____
_____

What did your mother think about it?

_____
_____
_____
_____

What is your most painful memory associated with money?

___

What's your financial worst-case scenario?

___

What do you value about money and what do you want it to do for you?

___

CHAPTER 3

HABITS WE HAVE FORMED

Get it gone!

READING TIME

As you read Chapter 3: "Habits We Have Formed" in *Finish Financially Free*, review, reflect on, and respond to the text by answering the following questions.

REFLECT AND TAKE ACTION:

What positive money habits do you currently have?

_____
_____
_____
_____
_____
_____

What negative money habits do you have?

_____
_____
_____
_____
_____
_____

Financially speaking, what do you allow in your life that doesn't align with your goals?

_____
_____
_____
_____
_____
_____
_____
_____

Of the list of non-financial habits provided in this chapter, are there any you need to work on or get rid of to radically alter your life?

_____
_____
_____
_____
_____

Follow the three steps in this chapter that will help you stop a bad habit more easily—write your answers to the steps below:

- Step 1:

_____
_____
_____
_____

- Step 2:

_____
_____
_____
_____

- Step 3:

_____
_____
_____
_____

Are you willing to do the work necessary to rid yourself of your bad habits—financial or otherwise? What will be your first action?

CHAPTER 4

COUPLES AND MONEY

*I believe that people don't fight about money.
I believe they fight about the use of money,
where it goes, and how it is spent and saved.*

READING TIME

As you read Chapter 4: "Couples and Money" in *Finish Financially Free*, review, reflect on, and respond to the text by answering the following questions.

REFLECT AND TAKE ACTION:

Do you and your partner see eye to eye when it comes to finances? If not, how do your perspectives differ? Remember, most couples are money opposites.

_____
_____
_____
_____
_____
_____
_____
_____

If you and your partner argue or fight about money, spending, or financial decisions, does it seem to be the same argument or fight over and over? What is the situation?

_____
_____
_____
_____
_____
_____
_____
_____

When was the last time you and your loved one sat down to discuss, create, and agree upon a financial plan? What's stopping you from doing this?

_____
_____
_____
_____
_____
_____
_____
_____
_____

Is there anything you wish your partner did or didn't do financially? Have you communicated this with them?

_____
_____
_____
_____
_____
_____
_____
_____
_____

Are you willing to compromise financially for you both to be content? Why or why not? Where do you need to compromise in your individual goals?

Are you able to see a new perspective to view money differently than you have in the past? Is there something you need to release emotionally that might allow you this new perspective?

How will you make your goals, your partner's goals, and your goals as a couple work?

_____
_____
_____
_____
_____
_____
_____
_____
_____
_____
_____
_____

Can you make this commitment to each other today, right now?

_____
_____
_____
_____
_____
_____
_____
_____
_____
_____

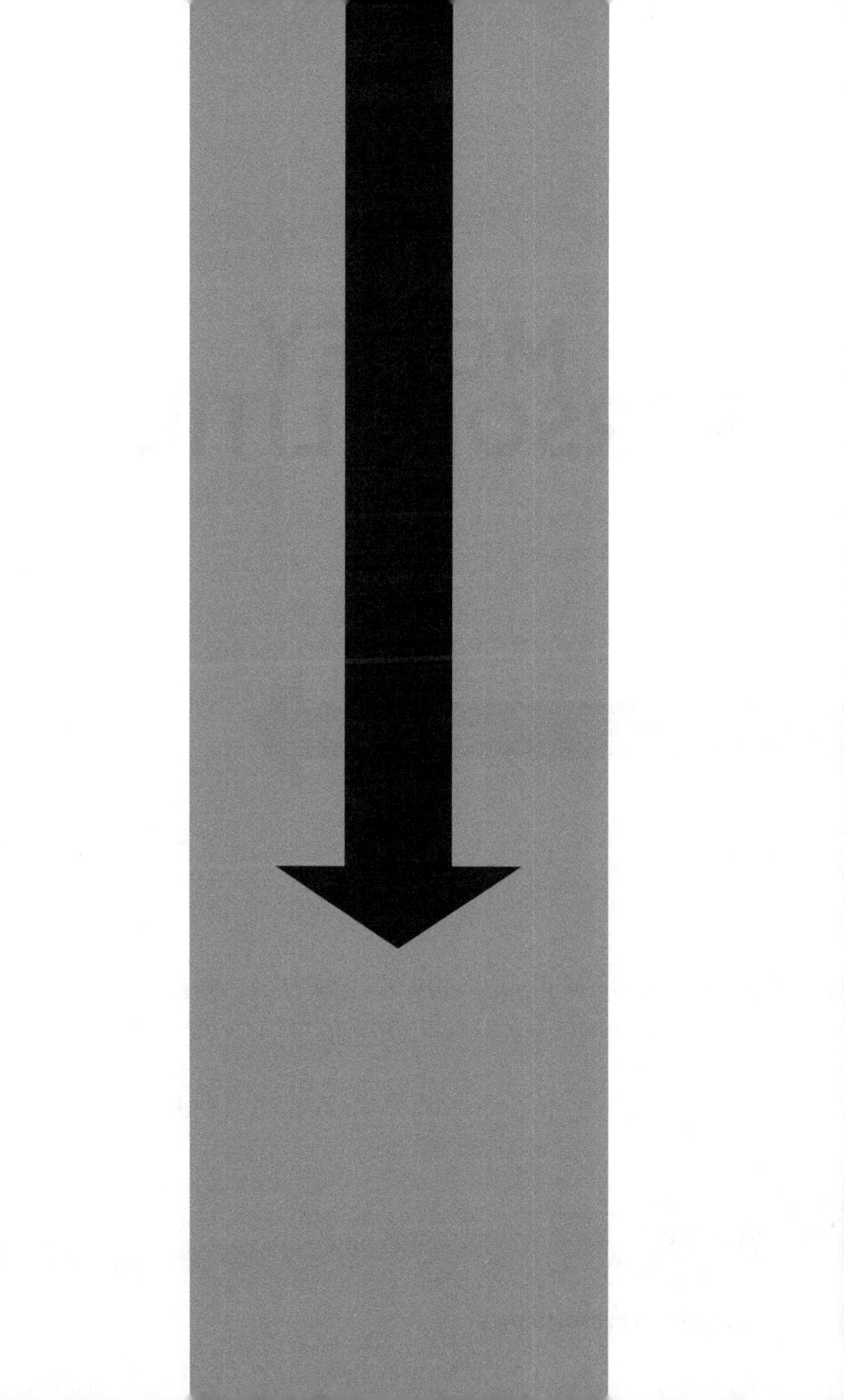

CHAPTER 5

MONEY PERSONALITIES

We have money personalities that express our beliefs and relationship with money.

READING TIME

As you read Chapter 5: "Money Personalities" in *Finish Financially Free*, review, reflect on, and respond to the text by answering the following questions.

REFLECT AND TAKE ACTION:

Of the different types of money personality types provided, which do you most identify with? What is your secondary attribute?

_____
_____
_____
_____
_____
_____
_____
_____
_____

What money personality would you say your partner is? Is there a secondary attribute? Do they agree?

_____
_____
_____
_____
_____
_____
_____
_____
_____
_____

How do you feel your money personality has changed over time? What caused this change?

_____
_____
_____
_____
_____
_____
_____
_____

How much money would satisfy you? Is there an object or amount of money that would create true happiness in your life?

_____
_____
_____
_____
_____
_____
_____
_____

What are the positives and negatives of your dominant money personality? Are any of these a surprise to you?

Are you content with your money personality, or do you want to change it? Explain your answer.

CHAPTER 6

PSYCHOLOGY IN MONEY

Psychology is tied to our money.

READING TIME

As you read Chapter 6: "Psychology in Money" in *Finish Financially Free*, review, reflect on, and respond to the text by answering the following questions.

REFLECT AND TAKE ACTION:

What stood out to you most about sunk cost and opportunity cost? Does knowing this change how you will make decisions by considering longer term goals?

_____
_____
_____
_____
_____
_____
_____
_____
_____
_____

Have you experienced loss aversion? What fear of loss where you trying to avoid?

_____
_____
_____
_____
_____
_____
_____
_____
_____
_____

What disrupters can you create to help your financial choices? How will you implement those disrupters in your life?

_____
_____
_____
_____
_____
_____
_____
_____
_____
_____
_____
_____
_____
_____
_____
_____
_____

What are some boundaries you can set today that will act as disrupters moving forward?

___

CHAPTER 7

THE BROKE TRAP

Tiny wins, compounded over time, create massive results.

READING TIME

As you read Chapter 7: "The Broke Trap" in *Finish Financially Free*, review, reflect on, and respond to the text by answering the following questions.

REFLECT AND TAKE ACTION:

In your own words, what is "The Broke Trap"? Have you ever fallen victim to this trap/cycle? Are you there now?

_____
_____
_____
_____
_____
_____
_____
_____
_____

What is your current total credit card debt? What is your rough plan for dealing with this debt?

_____
_____
_____
_____
_____
_____
_____
_____
_____
_____

How much money do you have in savings?

_____
_____
_____
_____
_____
_____
_____

What small actions and adjustments can you take that, when compounded over time, will have a big impact?

_____
_____
_____
_____
_____
_____
_____
_____

How much more of your budget can you put away into savings per month? How much more credit card debt could you comfortably pay down each month?

_____
_____
_____
_____
_____
_____
_____

What change are you willing to commit to in your life to avoid falling or staying victim to the broke trap?

_____
_____
_____
_____
_____
_____
_____
_____

CHAPTER 8

FINANCIAL LITERACY— THE BASICS

Once we can grasp what our beliefs about money are and how they kept us stuck, we can get into action to eliminate this needless stressor called debt.

READING TIME

As you read Chapter 8: "Financial Literacy—The Basics" in *Finish Financially Free*, review, reflect on, and respond to the text by answering the following questions.

REFLECT AND TAKE ACTION:

Do you consider yourself financially literate? Is there anything from the list of common mistakes that you struggle with?

_____
_____
_____
_____
_____
_____
_____

Which of the five main areas of money management (income, assets, debt, insurance, credit) do you most need to work on, and why?

_____
_____
_____
_____
_____
_____
_____
_____
_____
_____

Do you earn enough money? If not, how can you increase your value?

_____
_____
_____
_____
_____
_____

If you earn enough money, are you spending wisely? What area can you to cut back?

_____
_____
_____
_____
_____
_____

How much are you saving each month? Are you content with this number?

_____
_____

_____
_____
_____
_____
_____

How much do you invest each money? How could you grow this number?

_____
_____
_____
_____
_____

Do you have the appropriate insurance for you and your family? Is this a priority?

_____
_____
_____
_____
_____
_____
_____

CHAPTER 9

RUN YOUR NUMBERS LIKE YOU'RE A BUSINESS

If you find yourself getting overwhelmed or stuck, remind yourself that you are the CEO.

READING TIME

As you read Chapter 9: "Run Your Numbers Like You're a Business" in *Finish Financially Free*, review, reflect on, and respond to the text by answering the following questions.

REFLECT AND TAKE ACTION:

What would change about the way you run your numbers if you were a business? Would you look more intently at quarterly reports? Would you be more attentive to where you are losing money?

_____
_____
_____
_____
_____
_____
_____
_____

What are your top five financial goals to accomplish in the next one to three years?

_____
_____
_____
_____
_____
_____
_____
_____
_____

What needs to happen before these goals are met?

_____
_____
_____
_____
_____
_____
_____
_____

What will/can stand in the way of you achieving these goals?

_____
_____
_____
_____
_____
_____
_____
_____

Who or what will help you achieve these goals?

_____
_____
_____
_____
_____
_____
_____
_____

How will you celebrate these goals once you achieve them?

_____
_____
_____
_____
_____
_____
_____
_____

What are your top goals for over five years from now?

_____

_____

_____

_____

_____

_____

_____

_____

_____

_____

What needs to change or happen before this goal is met?

_____

_____

_____

_____

_____

_____

_____

_____

_____

_____

CHAPTER 10

CREDIT

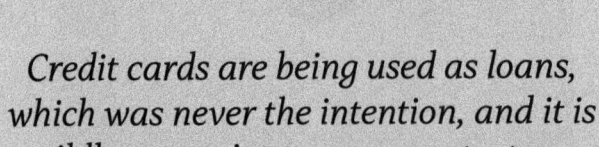

Credit cards are being used as loans, which was never the intention, and it is wildly expensive to use as a strategy.

READING TIME

As you read Chapter 10: "Credit" in *Finish Financially Free*, review, reflect on, and respond to the text by answering the following questions.

REFLECT AND TAKE ACTION:

How many credit cards do you have currently?

_____
_____
_____
_____
_____

What is the amount of debt on all of these cards combined? How does this make you feel?

_____
_____
_____
_____
_____
_____
_____
_____

To the best of your knowledge, what is your current credit score? What do you want your credit score to be?

_____
_____
_____
_____
_____
_____
_____

What did you learn about credit cards that you didn't already know in this chapter? How can you utilize this to more effectively use your credit card moving forward?

_____
_____
_____
_____
_____
_____
_____
_____
_____

Which of your credit cards are you going to start paying down to eliminate first: highest interest rate, highest balance or highest payment?

_____
_____
_____
_____
_____
_____
_____
_____
_____

CHAPTER 11

DEBT REPAYMENT

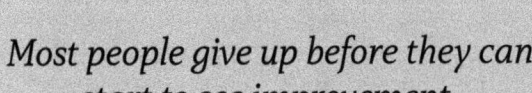

Most people give up before they can start to see improvement.

READING TIME

As you read Chapter 11: "Debt Repayment" in *Finish Financially Free*, review, reflect on, and respond to the text by answering the following questions.

REFLECT AND TAKE ACTION:

What did you learn about installment loans that you didn't know before?

_____
_____
_____
_____
_____
_____
_____

List out every installment loan and credit card you have with the balance and the payment. Did you already know the total amount of balances outstanding or did you just realize you owe a lot more than you thought?

_____
_____
_____
_____
_____
_____
_____
_____
_____
_____
_____

Now that you have your loans and credit card balances/payments, list in order which debt to start hyper-focusing on to pay off first, what will get paid next, etc. to set up your personalized debt-stacking strategy.

_____
_____
_____
_____
_____
_____
_____

On a scale of 1-10, how would you score yourself on how consistent you are at paying off your credit card balances on a consistent basis? How can you be even more consistent in paying off smaller credit card debt each month?

1   2   3   4   5   6   7   8   9   10

_____
_____
_____
_____
_____
_____
_____

Are you committing to paying installment loans with bi-weekly payments or extra principal payments moving forward to reduce interest?

How do you ensure you don't get into more debt? What boundaries have you set?

CHAPTER 12

CONSIDER YOUR FUTURE

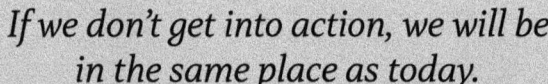

If we don't get into action, we will be in the same place as today.

READING TIME

As you read Chapter 12: "Consider Your Future" in *Finish Financially Free*, review, reflect on, and respond to the text by answering the following questions.

REFLECT AND TAKE ACTION:

Where do you want to be financially one year from now? In five years? In ten years? How are you preparing for these goals?

_____
_____
_____
_____
_____
_____
_____

Have you ever had the "lottery is my retirement" mindset? Why is this mindset ineffective and harmful?

_____
_____
_____
_____
_____
_____
_____
_____

Are the financial decisions you're making today moving you closer or farther from your goals?

_____
_____
_____
_____
_____
_____

Is your partner on board and able to stay on the trajectory toward your goals with you?

_____
_____
_____
_____
_____
_____

Do you invest in yourself? How?

_____
_____
_____

Are you surrounding yourself with financially like-minded people? What have they taught you?

Who can you need to add to your life as a mentor and accountability partner?

CHAPTER 13

ACTION PLAN

There is something amazing that happens when you write out your goals. It's no longer just a wish, it can now be formulated into a plan.

READING TIME

As you read Chapter 13: "Action Plan" in *Finish Financially Free*, review, reflect on, and respond to the text by answering the following questions.

REFLECT AND TAKE ACTION:

What about your money beliefs, personality, or habits needs to change?

_____
_____
_____
_____
_____
_____
_____

What is your current financial situation? How much debt are you in? How much are you earning? How much are you setting aside? How much are you investing? Take time to review credit card and bank statements and be brutally honest where you need to cut back, invest more, or adjust your spending.

_____
_____
_____
_____
_____
_____
_____
_____
_____

In one year from right now, where would you love to see your life? Have you paid off your credit card balances? Have you gotten that promotion or started with that other company that pays you better? Have you started your side hustle? What is different?

_____
_____
_____
_____
_____
_____
_____

If you only had twelve short months to accomplish the above items you listed, where would you start? Prioritize your time and focus.

_____
_____
_____
_____
_____
_____
_____

In three years from right now, where would you love to see your life? Are you in a job/career that you love? Are you growing in your industry? Where are you living? Are you maxing out your IRA and 401K contributions now that you have worked to eliminate your debt? Have you increased your savings rate to 10 percent with the goal of getting up to 20 percent?

_____
_____

_____

_____

_____

_____

In five years from now, where do you see your life? Who is in it? Is your debt eliminated? Are you a homeowner, if that is your goal? What other types of investments do you desire to have?

_____

_____

_____

_____

Do you have a checking and savings account? Is your savings account a high-yield savings account? Do you think you could benefit from an additional savings account to hide money away in?

_____

_____

_____

_____

A financial needs analysis (FNA) is an overview of your current and future financial position. Take time to follow the instructions in this chapter to create your unique FNA below:

Step 1: Understanding Your Money Story
- Go back and work through your money story if you have not done so.

Step 2: Understanding Your Current Numbers
- Complete your budget and highlight where you can cut some spending, make sure you start with your 5% savings in your numbers.

Step 3: Written Goals
- In one year from right now, where would you love to see your life? Have you paid off your credit card balances? Have you gotten that promotion or started with that other company that pays you better? Have you started your side hustle? Where are you living? Are you working out? Who is in your life? What is different? List out the top things that come to your mind and make you smile.

_____
_____
_____
_____
_____
_____
_____

- Next, create your debt stacking plan. What will you attack first? Next? Write it out!

Step 4: Your Checking and Savings Accounts

- Presuming you have each of these established, set up automated savings. Also, consider having multiple savings accounts, each labeled as your goal (emergency, house fund, etc.).

Step 5: Financial Needs Analysis

- Complete your FNA to see your expected income/expenses to start putting together your longer term savings goals.

Step 6: Create Your Savings Plan

- List how much margin you created by making some adjustments (roommate, overtime, part-time work, and paying off debt: $_____
- List how much you need to save monthly to hit your short-term goals: $_____
- Determine now, once you accomplish your short-term goals, if you can then move the monthly savings towards your long-term goals or if you are going to simultaneously start working toward your long-term goals.
- List how much you need to save monthly to hit your long-term goals: $_____
- An example of your long-term goals might be building passive income sources such as buying real estate or businesses.
- List out your savings number and timeline (example: $10,000 saved in 24 months = $416.67 a month). This is where you will start funding your dreams by moving over the money you were paying to debt (which is now eliminated through your debt stacking strategies) for maxing out retirement accounts, savings goals for short-term and long-term goals.

Step 7: Ideas to Create Passive Income

- List out your desires for passive income: real estate, owning REITs, stocks that pay dividends, businesses, etc.:

_____
_____
_____
_____

NOTES:

PERSONAL MONTHLY BUDGET

PERSONAL MONTHLY BUDGET

MONTHLY INCOME		
	Income (net, take home)	
	Extra/other income	
	Total monthly household	

HOUSING	Cost
Mortgage or rent	
Electricity	
Gas	
Water and sewer	
Lawn/Pool Care or Maintenance Costs	
Cable	
Waste removal	
Maintenance or repairs	
Supplies	
Alarm System	
Pest Control	
Home Improvement Projects	
Other	
SUBTOTALS	

TRANSPORTATION	Cost
Vehicle payment(s)	
Bus/taxi fare/Uber/Parking Fees/Tolls	
Insurance	
Licensing/Registration	

TRANSPORTATION	Cost
Fuel	
Maintenance (tires, oil, breaks, repairs)	
Other	
SUBTOTALS	

INSURANCE	Cost
Home	
Health	
Life	
Other (boat, umbrella, dental, flood)	
SUBTOTALS	

FOOD	Cost
Groceries	
Dining out	
Drive thrus, coffees, bottled water, misc	
SUBTOTALS	

PETS	Cost
Food	
Medical (vet visits & flea/heartworm)	
Grooming	
Toys	
Other	
SUBTOTALS	

PERSONAL CARE	Cost
Medical	
Hair/nails	
Clothing	
Dry cleaning/laundry	
Health club/gym	
Organization dues or fees	
Personal Items	
Other	
SUBTOTALS	

ENTERTAINMENT	Cost
Netflix/Hulu/Streaming	
Books/Audiobooks/CDs/Downloads	
Movies	
Concerts	
Sporting events	
Live theater	
Happy Hours/Drinks	
Babysitter costs so you can go out	
Subscription Services	
Software/Electronics	
Other	
SUBTOTALS	

LOANS	Cost
Personal	
Student	
Credit card	
Credit card	
Credit card	
Other	
SUBTOTALS	

REWARDS	Cost
Travel costs/savings towards	
Splurge	
Upgrades/Treats/New Shiny Item(s)	
Other (TV, cell phone, purse, watch)	
SUBTOTALS	

SAVINGS OR INVESTMENTS	Cost
Retirement account	
Retirement account	
Other	
SUBTOTALS	

GIFTS AND DONATIONS	Cost
Tithing	
Charity/Non-Profit	
Charity/Non-Profit	
SUBTOTALS	

OTHER	Cost
Childcare	
Professionals (therapist, lawyer, coach)	
Gifts (birthdays, anniversaries, baby)	
Child support, back taxes, interest	
Co-pays, deductibles, prescriptions	
Other	
SUBTOTALS	

TOTAL EXPENSES	

BALANCE (Total income minus total expenses)	

www.ingramcontent.com/pod-product-compliance
Lightning Source LLC
Chambersburg PA
CBHW062121080426
42734CB00012B/2940